I Love
Horses and Ponies

Nicola Jane Swinney

Sandy Creek
NEW YORK

Sandy Creek
NEW YORK

An Imprint of Sterling Publishing
387 Park Avenue South
New York, NY 10016

Text © 2014 by QEB Publishing, Inc.
Illustrations © 2014 by QEB Publishing, Inc.

This 2014 edition published by Sandy Creek.

ISBN 978-1-4351-5535-0

Manufactured in Guangdong, China
Lot #:
2 4 6 8 10 9 7 5 3 1
04/14

All images are courtesy
of Bob Langrish images.

In January 2011 Bob was
awarded an MBE (Member of the
Order of the British Empire) by the
Queen for Equestrian Photography and
Services to Art, having completely illustrated
around 150 books on horses. This award has
only ever been given to a handful of photographers
ever and no one specializing in equine photography.

Bob works for equine magazines in more than
20 countries and travels extensively all over the world
to obtain the 400,000 plus images in his library of pictures.

Contents

Words in **bold** are explained in the glossary.

Akhal-Teke

With a beautiful glowing coat, it is no wonder that the Akhal-Teke was popular with the rulers Alexander the Great and Genghis Khan, and with the explorer Marco Polo. This **breed** comes from Turkmenistan and was bred by the Teke tribe who lived in the Karakum Desert.

American Saddlebred

As its name suggests, this beautiful creature was bred to be a very comfortable ride. During the Civil War, it was the horse of choice of the generals and, when the war ended, the horse's popularity spread across the entire United States.

Appaloosa

The Native Americans were very proud of their spotted horses. The Nez Perce tribe lived along the banks of the Palouse River in Idaho and bred horses with striking coat patterns. They became known as Appaloosa and eventually became an American icon.

Arabian

The Arabian is one of the world's oldest breeds and was tamed by travelers in the Arabian deserts. Today, they are used as racehorses and riding horses. They are known for their speed, intelligence, and good nature, and are found all over the world.

11

Australian Stock Horse/Waler

Horses were on the first 11 British ships to sail to Australia in 1788. These horses were a mix of Thoroughbred, Arabian, and Spanish stock and only the strongest survived the tough journey. The survivors became the first Australian Stock Horses.

13

Barb

Some believe the Godolphin Arabian was actually a Barb— a breed from North Africa that is thought to share a common ancestor with the Arabian. Prized by the Berber people of North Africa, it was an exceptional **warhorse**, combining great speed with incredible **endurance**.

15

Belgian

Although the Belgian is a heavy horse, it is also handsome. Bred from the huge Flemish horse, which was known to be in Europe during the time of Julius Caesar, the Belgian loved the country's lush and fertile soil. The Belgian people are right to be proud of their magnificent horse.

Boer Pony

Boer is a Dutch word for "farmer." When Dutch settlers landed on the Cape of Good Hope, South Africa, they took with them their small, **hardy**, and nimble horses. Originally from Indonesia, the horse was prized for its stamina and sure-footedness.

Brumby

There is some mystery as to how Australia's wild horse got its name. An English settler named James Brumby allowed his horses to wander free, and when someone asked to whom they belonged, they were told, "they're Brumby's." Sadly, the horses are seen as pests by farmers.

21

Camargue

Known as "the horses of the sea," Camargues roam like ghosts along the edge of the Rhône River where it meets the Mediterranean Sea. Camargue horses are always white—or, more correctly, light gray—but are born black or dark brown and lighten with age.

23

Caspian

These tiny horses were only discovered in the 1960s, living by the Caspian Sea in what is now northern Iran. However, the Caspian is thought to be a very old breed, with evidence of small horses existing as early as 3000 BC.

25

Chincoteague

These rare **feral** ponies live on Assateague Island off the East Coast of the United States. We do not know exactly how the ponies got to the island, but they may have been shipwrecked there hundreds of years ago.

Cleveland Bay

As its name suggests, this breed is from the Cleveland area of northeast England and is always bay in color—a rich reddish brown with black points. It was bred to be a **coaching horse** but is today used by the British royal family for ceremonial duties.

Clydesdale

A similar type to the
Shire, the Clydesdale
was influenced by
a Flemish horse
imported to Scotland
by the Sixth Duke of Hamilton.
He allowed the **stallion** to breed
with his tenants' **mares**. A colt
named Glancer, or Thompson's
Black Horse, was the first
official Clydesdale.

Connemara

The west coast of Ireland is wild and craggy, so the ponies who lived there had to be hardy and sure-footed. The Connemara, Ireland's only native breed, was bred to be tough and strong. But it is also very good-looking and kind, which makes it an enjoyable ride.

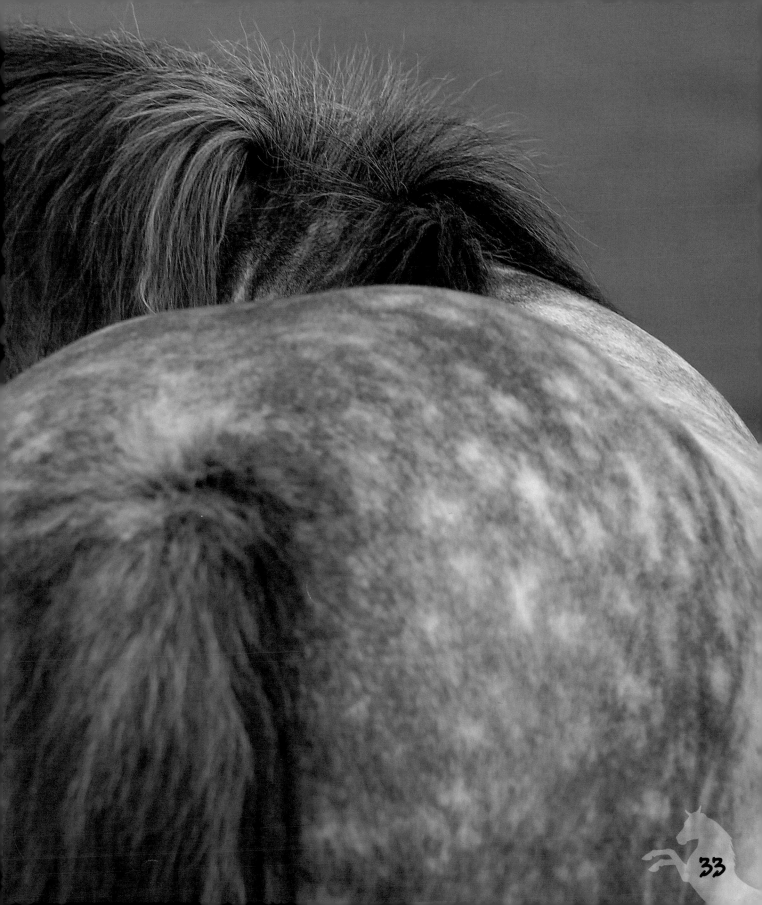

33

Criollo

Originally from Spanish stock, the Criollo was brought to Argentina by Pedro de Mendoza, the founder of the city of Buenos Aires. The breed is famous for its stamina. The very first horses lived in a tough environment, but by 1580, the feral horse population was around 12,000.

Dales/Fell

Pack ponies were used to carry coal, lead, copper, and wool across northern England. The sure-footed Dales and Fell ponies—similar, but recognized as separate breeds—were ideal. Despite being small, they were strong and could carry heavy weights for long distances.

Dartmoor

Like the Exmoor, the Dartmoor pony is well adapted to its moorland environment and is hardy and tough. They have been used to work in the tin mines of southwest England and, because of their natural speed and **agility**, are perfect for playing polo.

Exmoor

Horses crossed into the British Isles 100,000 years ago when the islands were joined with Europe. When the English Channel formed, around 7,000 years ago, they were trapped. The ponies of Exmoor in Devon are therefore very **pure**.

Falabella

A perfect horse in miniature, the Falabella has been bred for centuries. It was originally bred from Spanish horses brought to Argentina in the 1500s. They were turned loose and left to fend for themselves. The smaller horses coped well on the wide, flat, grassy plains of Argentina.

Fjord

There have been wild horses in Scandinavia since the Ice Age. Viking burial grounds show that horses had been bred by man for at least 2,000 years. Norway's Fjord breed is thought to have been developed from these early horses, making it a very old breed.

Friesian

One of the oldest breeds in Europe, the Friesian was used as a warhorse. Roman historians found evidence of Friesians being used at Hadrian's Wall in Britain in around 150 AD. Known as the black pearl of the Netherlands, it has added to British breeds such as the Fell and Dales.

47

Gelderlander

Friesian blood was used to found the Gelderlander. Developed as a **carriage horse**, it could also work the land if needed. Still bred in the Netherlands today, it is a very good competition horse.

Haflinger

A very attractive breed, the Haflinger has a glowing coat of gold that varies from light **palomino** to rich chestnut. It has a light mane and tail. It was based on the native horses of the Austrian Tyrol Mountains, which were crossed with Arabian stock.

Hanoverian

Germany's magnificent **warmblood** is renowned the world over for its beauty, power, and agility. It was first bred by George II, the King of England, in 1735. It was originally used as a high-class carriage horse and now competes in almost all horse sports.

Highland

Hardy as well as beautiful, the Highland is a great favorite of Queen Elizabeth II, who breeds them under her Balmoral name. The Highland is one of the biggest of the United Kingdom's native breeds, as well as one of the oldest.

55

Icelandic

The people of Iceland have no word for "pony" so their sturdy little pony is called a horse. It has two extra **gaits**: the tölt, a fast-running walk; and the skold, a sprint, which allows it to cover short distances at speeds of up to 30 mph (48 kph).

Konik-Tarpan

The Konik is a very old breed from Poland. It shares basic characteristics with the ancient Tarpan and is being used to recreate the **extinct** breed. The last Tarpan died in 1876 but it could be found across Europe and Russia from around 3000 BC.

59

Lipizzaner

Famed the world over as the "dancing white horses" of the Spanish Riding School in Vienna, the majestic Lipizzaner is based on **Iberian** horses. However, it was originally bred for battle, not ballet. The school traditionally keeps one dark-colored horse along with the gray ones.

Mangalarga Marchador

The national horse of Brazil was based on a stallion name "Sublime"—and sublime perfectly describes this horse. The "marcha" part of its name relates to its gait, which is smooth and rhythmic. The breed has been kept pure for more than 180 years.

63

Marwari

The distinctive little curled
ears of the Marwari show
its Arabian history. It was
originally from India, where
it was treated as superior
to humans—even the royal
family! It was once a warhorse
and was known for its
homing instinct.

65

Mérens

Similar to Britain's Dales and Fell ponies, the Mérens is a tough little creature, with a coal-black coat. It is used by the mountain farmers of the Ariège region of France. The farmers turn the Mérens out for the summer so the ponies return to their natural herd instincts.

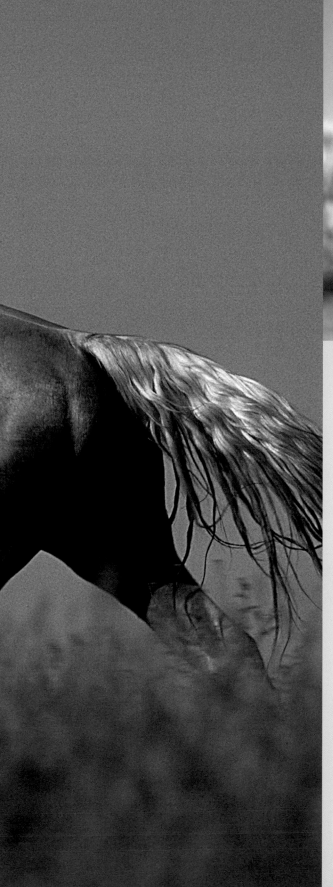

Missouri Fox Trotter

This horse takes its charming name from its gait—a fluid, four-beat "fox trot" in which it appears to walk with its front legs and **trot** with its back legs. As a result, the rider feels very little jarring. The breed is gentle and can be used for almost any job.

Morgan

Horses were often known by the name of their owner, so when word spread of a good-looking, fast, and incredibly strong horse, it soon became known as the "Justin Morgan horse." The stallion's name was "Figure," and it was the founding **sire** of this horse breed.

Mustang

The Mustang is America's best-known horse. It is the ancestor of the horses brought to the New World by the conquistadors in the 16th century. Some of those horses escaped, or were set free, and became wild. The Mustang often has a grayish-**dun** coloring called "**grullo**."

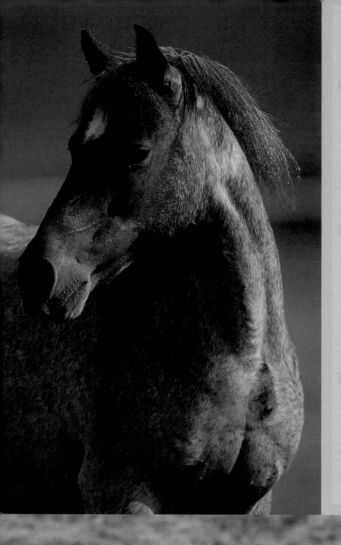

New Forest

The great forests of England once belonged to the King or Queen and were used as royal hunting grounds. In 1016, rights to **graze** in the New Forest were granted to "commoners" and they still hold that right. The ponies are rounded up every year in groups to check on their well-being.

75

Orlov Trotter

One of the world's most attractive horse breeds, the Orlov Trotter was developed to cross the huge Russian landscape quickly and easily. Catherine the Great of Russia gave land to Count Alexei Orlov, who bred the trotter based on Arabian stock.

Palomino

This is one of the most beautiful of all breeds. Its coat glows like a newly minted gold coin and is set off by a white mane and tail. These horses can be found all over the world, but the Palomino is only recognized as a breed in the United States.

Paso Fino

Its name means "fine step" and the description certainly fits this lovely creature, which is famous for its gait. But it is just as well-known for its beauty and its grace. It is muscular and compact, with a graceful head and arching neck.

Percheron

Perhaps France's best-known breed, the splendid Percheron takes its name from La Perche, a region in the center of France. It is an ancient breed and was used as a warhorse, carrying knights in full armor. Arabian blood has since been added to make it less heavy.

83

Peruvian Paso

The Peruvian Paso is similar in many ways to the Paso Fino, but they are two separate breeds. The Peruvian Paso is sweet-natured and has a unique and graceful gait called the "**termino**." It is a comfortable ride.

Pony of the Americas

A colt was born with an unusual black handprint marking and so its owner named it "Black Hand."

America's favorite pony descended from this colt.

PRE/Iberian

Iberia's magnificent horses are almost as important, in breeding terms, as the Arabian. The Lusitano, from Portugal, and the Spanish Andalusian are known as the Pura Raza Español (PRE). *Pura Raza* means "pure blood" in Spanish. The two horses are very similar.

Przewalski's Horse

The last truly wild horse still alive today is named for Colonel Nicolai Przewalski. The Colonel recorded herds of **primitive** horses in the mountains of Mongolia in 1879. Przewalski's Horse is unique in that it has 66 chromosomes—the "template" of all living things— while other breeds have 64.

Quarter Horse

This speedy breed got its name because it could sprint distances of a quarter of a mile (half a kilometer) and men placed bets on who had the fastest horse. It is said that some of the great **plantations** of the American Deep South were won and lost because of bets placed on these races!

93

Rocky Mountain Horse

From the state of Kentucky, these beautiful and clever horses are safe and comfortable to ride. They love human company and were used to take riders of all ages through the Natural Bridge State Park in Kentucky.

94

95

Selle Français

The word *selle* means "saddle" in French, and this handsome horse was bred to be ridden. Local French stock was bred with Thoroughbreds, Arabians, and trotters, and no other blood was introduced to keep the breed pure. It now competes in all **equestrian** events.

97

Shetland

The tiny Shetland is named for the Scottish islands. It is an ancient breed. There is evidence that these ponies have been on the islands since the Bronze Age (3200-600 BC). The Shetland has adapted to a harsh climate and can survive every kind of weather.

Shire

One of the biggest horses in the world, the massive Shire is a gentle giant. It was used as a warhorse and King Henry VIII of England was said to be a fan. A Shire named "Duke" was measured at 19.3 **hands** at the shoulder—that's 6 feet 5 inches (2 m)!

Sorraia

A rather plain little horse, the Sorraia was used to herd the wild bulls of Iberia. It takes its name from two rivers, the Sor and the Raia. Its **DNA** has been found in the American Mustang and it has contributed to many breeds, including the PRE.

Standardbred

Trotting races were popular in America in the late 1700s and were almost always one mile (1.5 km) long. The Standardbred was developed to race this distance in a set time. Races were run along city roads, and many cities still have a Race Street today.

Suffolk

This tough little horse is sometimes called the Suffolk Punch, because of its chunky appearance. It is always chestnut in color and, for a **draft** breed, is very attractive. It is hardy and strong, but also intelligent.

Tennessee Walking Horse

The first breed to bear the name of an American state, the Tennessee Walker was popular with owners of southern plantations. Using a comfortable "running walk," it could reach speeds of up to 20 mph (32 kph).

Thoroughbred

Modern Thoroughbreds whizz around the world's racetracks. They can trace their **ancestry** back to three stallions: the Godolphin Arabian, the Darley Arabian, and the Byerley Turk. These three stallions were used to start what is now the multibillion-dollar horse racing industry.

Trakehner

When King Wilhelm of Prussia decided to breed a superb cavalry mount, he selected the very best horses from his seven Royal **Studs** and moved them to the green pastures of Trakehnen in 1732. The **studbook** remains closed to make sure the Trakehner breed is kept pure.

Welsh Section A/B

Julius Caesar brought **oriental**-type horses to the British Isles when he invaded. Their influence can be seen in the Welsh Mountain Pony (Section A of the Welsh studbook) in its elegant, dished face. The Welsh Section B is slightly bigger and finer than the Section A.

115

Welsh Section C/D

The Welsh Cob (Section D) has the same elegant head as the Section A but it is much bigger and there is no upper height limit. The Welsh Pony of Cob Type (Section C) must stand no taller than 13.2 hands (4 feet 6 inches, 1.5 m).

Glossary

Ancestry
Family history

Agility
Being able to move quickly and easily

Breed
A group of animals of a similar type, with clearly defined characteristics

Carriage/coaching horse
A horse used to pull a carriage or a coach. They were generally good-looking as well as strong

Coldblood
The name given to the heavy draft-type breeds, such as the Shire

DNA
The material of which all living things are made

Draft
A heavy horse breed, such as shire

Dun
A sandy coat color, usually with black mane and tail and markings

Endurance
Able to continue even when tired, wet, cold, and hungry

Equestrian
To do with horses and riding

Extinct
No longer in existence, disappeared altogether

Feral
A domesticated animal that has returned to the wild. The American Mustang, for example, is feral rather than wild

Gait
The horse or pony's movements, including walk, trot, canter, and gallop as well as the movements of five-gaited breeds, such as some American horses

Graze
To feed on growing grass or pasture

Grullo
A grayish-dun color, considered primitive

Hardy
Able to endure tiredness, hardship, and exposure to harsh weather

Hand
The traditional measurement used for horses and ponies—a hand is four inches

Hotblood
Breeds such as the Arab and the Thoroughbred are said to be hotblooded—characterized by fine bones, thin coat, and high spirits

Iberia
The area including Spain and Portugal

Mare
A female horse or pony aged four and over

Oriental
Horses originating from Central or West Asia, including the Arab and the Barb

Palomino
A color: rich golden coat with light mane and tail. It is regarded as a breed in the United States

Plantation
Huge farms or estates, particularly found in the south of the United States and often growing cotton, coffee, or sugar

Primitive
Being the first or earliest of the kind in existence

Pure
A horse or pony that has two parents of the same breed

Sire
A horse's father

Stallion
A male horse that has not been castrated

Stud
A farm in which horses are kept for breeding

Studbook
A book that records the pedigrees of horses. A closed studbook does not accept any outside blood (from other breeds)

Termino
The unique gait of the Peruvian Paso. The horse moves its front legs in a rolling motion similar to a swimmer doing front crawl

Trot
A two-beat gait in which the lateral (diagonal) front and hind legs move together

Warhorse
An horse used by cavalry in battles during war

Warmblood
a horse that has both **hotblood** and **coldblood** in its ancestry

Ponies

Boer Pony
Connemara
Criollo
Dales/Fell
Dartmoor
Exmoor
Fjord
Haflinger
Highland
Icelandic
Konik-Tarpan
Mérens
New Forest
Pony of the Americas
Shetland
Welsh section A/B
Welsh section C/D

Horses

Akhal-Teke
American Saddlebred
Appaloosa
Arabian
Australian Stock
  Horse/Waler
Barb
Brumby
Camargue
Caspian
Chincoteague
Cleveland Bay
Falabella
Friesian
Gelderlander
Hanoverian
Lipizzaner
Mangalarga Marchador
Marwari
Missouri Fox Trotter

Morgan
Mustang
Orlov Trotter
Palomino
Paso Fino
Peruvian Paso
PRE/Iberian
Przewalski's Horse
Quarter Horse
Rocky Mountain Horse
Selle Français
Standardbred
Sorraia
Tennessee Walking Horse
Thoroughbred
Trakehner

Draft Horses

Clydesdale
Belgian
Percheron
Shire
Suffolk

Draft Horse
Up to 19HH
(76 inches/193cm)
and heavily built

1 hand
(HH)
=
4 inches
(10 cm)

Horse
Above 14.2HH
(58 inches/148cm)

Pony
Up to 14.2HH
(58 inches/148cm)

Child
11HH
(44 inches/
111cm)